A LifeBuilder

GOOD & EVIL

8 studies
for individuals or groups

Douglas Connelly

with notes for leaders

Getting the Most Out of
Good and Evil

Where is God when terrorists attack or when massive tsunamis sweep away thousands of people? When children die from cancer or our sweet grandmothers lose their memories of us, we want to know if God knows what is going on—and if he really cares. We want to know why he doesn't redirect a destructive hurricane or do something to prevent a famine or let the police find a serial rapist before another victim suffers.

Our questions get more personal when a drunk driver injures a friend or a convenience store robbery in our neighborhood turns deadly. How can human beings be so careless—or murderous?

The most painful questions come when we look at our own hearts and see what thoughts or impulses lurk in the dark corners. Where does that evil come from and how do we overcome its powerful drag on our lives?

Why Bad Things Happen in God's World

When we turn to the Bible, we find some startling news! Evil is a very real force in our world and in our lives, but God is not surprised by evil. When disasters happen, God is there. He is not the source of evil, but he sovereignly rules over a world that chooses to ignore him. We also discover that God can take the worst event and bring good from it.

We will explore some of these issues of good and evil in this study guide. We won't find all the answers because God doesn't give us all the answers. Instead we will learn to trust

God and his sovereign power even in the darkest days of pain and suffering.

Suggestions for Individual Study

1. As you begin each study, pray that God will speak to you through his Word.

2. Read the introduction to the study and respond to the personal reflection question or exercise. This is designed to help you focus on God and on the theme of the study.

3. Each study deals with a particular passage—so that you can delve into the author's meaning in that context. Read and reread the passage to be studied. The questions are written using the language of the New International Version, so you may wish to use that version of the Bible. The New Revised Standard Version is also recommended.

4. This is an inductive Bible study, designed to help you discover for yourself what Scripture is saying. The study includes three types of questions. *Observation* questions ask about the basic facts: who, what, when, where and how. *Interpretation* questions delve into the meaning of the passage. *Application* questions help you discover the implications of the text for growing in Christ. These three keys unlock the treasures of Scripture.

Write your answers to the questions in the spaces provided or in a personal journal. Writing can bring clarity and deeper understanding of yourself and of God's Word.

5. It might be good to have a Bible dictionary handy. Use it to look up any unfamiliar words, names or places.

6. Use the prayer suggestion to guide you in thanking God for what you have learned and to pray about the applications that have come to mind.

7. You may want to go on to the suggestion under "Now or Later," or you may want to use that idea for your next study.

Suggestions for Members of a Group Study

1. Come to the study prepared. Follow the suggestions for individual study mentioned above. You will find that careful preparation will greatly enrich your time spent in group discussion.

2. Be willing to participate in the discussion. The leader of your group will not be lecturing. Instead, he or she will be encouraging the members of the group to discuss what they have learned. The leader will be asking the questions that are found in this guide.

3. Stick to the topic being discussed. Your answers should be based on the verses which are the focus of the discussion and not on outside authorities such as commentaries or speakers. These studies focus on a particular passage of Scripture. Only rarely should you refer to other portions of the Bible. This allows for everyone to participate in in-depth study on equal ground.

4. Be sensitive to the other members of the group. Listen attentively when they describe what they have learned. You may be surprised by their insights! Each question assumes a variety of answers. Many questions do not have "right" answers, particularly questions that aim at meaning or application. Instead the questions push us to explore the passage more thoroughly.

When possible, link what you say to the comments of others. Also, be affirming whenever you can. This will encourage some of the more hesitant members of the group to participate.

5. Be careful not to dominate the discussion. We are sometimes so eager to express our thoughts that we leave too little opportunity for others to respond. By all means participate! But allow others to also.

6. Expect God to teach you through the passage being discussed and through the other members of the group. Pray that you will have an enjoyable and profitable time together, but also that as a result of the study you will find ways that you can take action individually and/or as a group.

7. Remember that anything said in the group is considered confidential and should not be discussed outside the group unless specific permission is given to do so.

8. If you are the group leader, you will find additional suggestions at the back of the guide.

1

Understanding the Human Condition

Romans 3:9-20

It takes a strong stomach to watch the nightly news or to pick up a newspaper. Bad news is everywhere! Terrorist threats, child abductions, financial scandals, corruption in high places—it makes you wonder what the real problem, the deeper problem, in human culture is. Is it just a person or two gone bad, or is it a more pervasive issue—a problem residing in each of us?

GROUP DISCUSSION. How do you respond to the bad news in our world—and where do you look for good news?

PERSONAL REFLECTION. What kinds of "bad news" reports bother you most deeply? What questions do those reports prompt about God?

The Bible makes it clear that the fundamental problem in human society is in each human heart and mind. We live in a world that is marked by sin. Our hearts are alienated from God by our own choices. We are born with a bent toward evil that no amount of education or resolution can ever overcome. The only hope we have is for a transformation in our lives by the power of God. *Read Romans 3:9-20.*

1. If this were the only passage of God's Word that we possessed, how would you feel after reading it?

2. Before the apostle Paul shares the good news of our redemption in Christ, he gives us the bad news that every person is separated from God and is incapable of meeting the holy standard that God requires. Why is it so important to Paul to hammer home that point?

How does our culture respond to the ideas of personal sinfulness and separation from God?

3. Based on verses 10-18, how would you characterize human thought?

Human speech?

Human actions?

4. How would you explain this passage to a person who believes he or she is basically good and not guilty of any serious sin before God?

5. In verse 11 Paul says that there is "no one who seeks God." But don't those who are Christians seek after God when they believe in Jesus? How would you explain Paul's statement?

6. A popular explanation of this passage in Romans goes like this: "Not every person is as bad as they could be, but every person is as bad off in relation to God as they could be." Do you agree with that assertion? Why or why not?

7. Can we be made right with God by trying our hardest to keep the Ten Commandments? Explain your answer.

8. If human beings are really as far from God as Paul affirms, how can we ever hope for anything good to happen in our world?

---

9. How does an understanding of God's grace set you free from the burden of trying to gain God's approval by keeping his law?

Describe how you have been made right (or hope to be made right) with God?

Thank God that he loved us and provided redemption for us when we were spiritually dead and separated from him.

Now or Later

Each of Paul's declarations in verses 10-18 comes directly from the Old Testament. Read the following passages to see where Paul got some of his material: Psalm 14:1-3; Psalm 36:1-4; and Isaiah 59:1-13.

What additional insights do these passage provide about the human condition apart from God's transforming grace?

2

Dealing with Disaster

Job 1

My friend John had an argument with his son one morning just before the boy left for school. It was a silly argument over a trivial matter, but the boy left before the issue could be resolved. His mother was waiting to drive him to school, and if he took any longer, she would be late for work.

Thirty minutes later the phone call came. On the way to school a truck skidded through an intersection and hit his family's car. His wife and his son were both killed.

The argument still plays in John's mind—and he still remembers the terrible feeling that hit him when the police officer's call came.

GROUP DISCUSSION. What situation have you experienced or heard about recently that produced unexplained suffering or pain? What questions did you want to ask God?

PERSONAL REFLECTION. How do you usually respond to natural or human disaster? Who or what do you hold responsible for such events?

Job was a good and godly man who suffered incredible loss and tragedy—all to settle a contest between God and Satan! We can hardly believe what we read because we aren't sure we could respond to such loss in the same way. *Read Job 1.*

1. The scenes of the book of Job unfold like a drama. Mark off the scenes in heaven and the scenes on Earth in this chapter. Who are the main characters in each?

2. Why is it significant that God initiates Job's testing by bringing up Job's name first?

3. How does Satan think Job will respond to God's testing, and why does he think Job will respond that way (vv. 9-11)?

4. God puts clear limitations on Satan toward Job (verse 12). What does that tell you about Satan's power in your life?

4. How might the work of God be displayed in such circumstances even if the person is not made whole or healed?

---

5. Why does Jesus make mud and smear it on the man's eyes and send him to a different location? Why not just instantly heal the man?

---

6. If situations of disability do not always arise from specific sins, how can we explain their presence in our world?

---

7. In Exodus 4:11 God says this to Moses: "Who gave man his mouth? Who makes him deaf or mute? Who gives him sight or makes him blind? Is it not I, the LORD?" Can God be good and still make that statement? Explain your answer.

8. Based on what we've learned in this study, what can you say to the parents of a Down syndrome child or to a girl born with a deformed face about God's involvement in their condition?

---

9. How can you respond like Jesus did to people God brings across your path who are disabled or who suffer from some difficult deformity?

Give thanks for a God who is good. Even when we cannot fully understand how he works, we can have confidence in his goodness—all the time.

Now or Later

Plan a group outing to a nursing home or to a mental health group home or to the pediatric ward of a hospital. Talk to the directors of the facility about how you can bring comfort and cheer into the lives of the people you visit. Make your time there a blessing for each person you encounter.

4

Struggling
with Sickness

James 5:13-18

We knew our three-year-old son was sick, but we didn't know
how seriously until the doctor called. We had taken Kyle to the
doctor's office because he had the flu. Now our pediatrician
told us to take him to the emergency room as quickly as we
could and that she would meet us there. What started as the flu
left Kyle severely dehydrated and on the verge of major organ
failure. As our family and friends were notified, they began to
surround Kyle with prayer. Intravenous feeding, close monitor-
ing, medical attention and God's intervention brought him to
full recovery.

GROUP DISCUSSION. Tell the group about a time when you or a
close family member was sick. What emotions did you sense as
you passed through that experience?

PERSONAL REFLECTION. What do you do first when you get
sick? Do you ever pray to be healed?

In his very practical New Testament letter James gives some clear direction about how Christians are to handle serious sickness. His instructions may sound strange to us but it's an approach God has promised to bless. *Read James 5:13-18.*

1. As you look through the passage again, what indicators can you find that these instructions are for Christians to follow and not general commands to everyone?

2. James uses a word in verse 14 translated "sick" that means without strength for recovery. What does that tell you about when these instructions might apply to you?

3. The sick person is to call the elders of the church to prayer and anointing. The "elders" in the New Testament were those in spiritual leadership among the local group of Christians. Who would you call in this situation?

What would you say to them?

4. Some interpreters of James believe the oil is a reference to medicine or medical treatment. Others believe the oil is a symbol of dependence on the Holy Spirit. Which view do you think is better and what statements from the passage lead you to that conclusion?

5. Does James "guarantee" physical healing if we follow these instructions? Explain your answer.

6. Why does James connect physical healing with the confession of sin?

7. If we confess our sins to God, isn't that enough? Why confess them to each other?

8. "The prayer of a righteous person is powerful and effective" (v. 16 TNIV). How will that statement and the example of Elijah (vv. 17-18) affect the way you pray after this for a person who is sick?

9. How can you use this passage to help a Christian who is seriously ill?

What will you do if that person chooses not to follow the Bible's direction?

Offer your prayers to the Lord who is the great Healer.

Now or Later

Read the account in 1 Kings 18:41-46 of Elijah's prayer for the return of rain after a three-year drought in Israel. Glean out two or three aspects of Elijah's prayer life that are most striking to you. How can you cultivate these qualities in your own personal practice of prayer?

5

Our Enemy
in the World

Revelation 12:7-12

The little kid standing at my door with a plastic pumpkin bucket was dressed in a bright red suit with red horns, a long pointed tail and a blow-up pitchfork in his hand. "And who are you?" I asked as I opened the door to pass out the treats. "I'm the devil!" he said with mock glee in his voice. As he jumped off the front step to join his dad on the sidewalk, I thought how nice it would be if the devil were really that harmless.

GROUP DISCUSSION. How do you envision the devil? Describe your perception of him to the group.

PERSONAL REFLECTION. When have you felt oppressed or attacked by evil? How did you respond to that assault?

One major source of evil in our world is the activity of a personal, powerful being who is totally committed to his opposition to God on every issue. The Bible calls that evil being Satan or the devil. As the apostle John wrote the book of Revelation, he saw a stunning scene unfold before him—a scene of warfare in heaven. *Read Revelation 12:7-12.*

1. As you scan through the passage again, do you think this scene took place in the past, that it will take place in the future, or that it is going on right now in the present? What clues from the text lead you to that conclusion?

2. Holy angels ("Michael and his angels") fight against evil angels ("the dragon and his angels") and the evil angels are defeated. What are they fighting over?

3. Five names or descriptions are used for the leader of the evil angels in verse 9. What insight does each name give you about the character of this being?
• The great dragon:

• That ancient serpent (see Genesis 3:1-15):

• The devil (= the slanderer):

• Satan (= the accuser):

• Who leads the whole world astray:

4. What role might Satan play in the evil and suffering in the world today?

5. Why doesn't God just eliminate Satan right now?

6. If Satan were eliminated, would evil cease to exist? Why or why not?

7. In verse 10 Satan is called "the accuser of our brothers." What insight does that phrase give you into how Satan might be involved in your life?

8. What resources do Christians have at their disposal to overcome Satan's accusations and attacks (v. 11)?

9. What can you do to become stronger in the spiritual battle against Satan?

How can you pray for Christian friends or family members who are facing spiritual battles?

Speak openly with the Lord about the spiritual battles you face, keeping in mind that the one who lives in you is greater than the one who is in the world.

Now or Later

The Bible gives us some practical help for defending ourselves against Satan's assaults. Read the following passages and write out some ways that you can apply their instructions to your life.

James 4:7

Ephesians 6:10-11

1 Corinthians 10:13

1 John 4:4

6

The Enemy Within

The man sitting across the table from me was a good friend, a leader in his church and a deeply loved member of his family. He ran a successful business and gave generously to those in need. I've known very few people who had a greater desire to follow Christ wholeheartedly. But my friend was struggling. One area of his life seemed impossible to bring into submission to Christ. He would determine to walk in obedience to the Lord and would succeed for a while, but then some crisis would push him back over the edge. He was on the verge of despair.

GROUP DISCUSSION. What advice would you give this man? What kind of advice would probably do more harm than good?

PERSONAL REFLECTION. In what areas do you struggle most with obedience to the Lord? What do you say to yourself when you fail?

Romans 7 has generated more debate than almost any other section of Paul's writing. Some students of the book believe Paul is talking about his life before he believed in Jesus—the days when he was a law-keeping Pharisee. Other interpreters think Paul is describing life as a disobedient Christian who is far from God. The third view is that Paul is talking about the struggles we have in the normal Christian life. I think this view fits best with what Paul says. We have a desire to obey God and live holy lives, but there is a powerful force in us that works against that desire. The old nature, the tattered remnants of the old way of life, can sometimes grip us with incredible strength. *Read Romans 7:14-25.*

---

1. Do you think Paul is being too hard on himself in this passage, or is he just being realistic? Explain your answer.

---

2. When Paul hears God's law, he has a desire to obey it but ends up disobeying. What reasons does Paul give for doing what he does *not* want to do (vv. 15-17)?

---

3. Is Paul just trying to blame someone or something else for his failure when he says, "It is no longer I who do it, but it is sin living in me that does it" (vv. 17, 20)? Why or why not?

4. Give an example of how you have sensed the struggle in your own life between the two forces—a desire to do good and the law of sin at work within your members (vv. 21-24).

5. Where does Paul look for help to be delivered from his struggle (vv. 24-25)?

When and how do you think that deliverance will come?

6. If the final victory over sin's power only comes when we are delivered from "this body of death," what can we do in the meantime—give up? try harder? Explain your answer.

7. What can you say to a Christian friend who is struggling with some area of disobedience that will give him or her hope and help in the struggle?

8. Based on this passage, what will you do when the pressure to sin against God builds up in your life?

---

9. What can you do to remind yourself of God's empowerment in your life to live in obedience to him?

Pray that God the Holy Spirit will help you to "put to death" the old life and then to "clothe yourself" with Christlikeness day after day (Colossians 3:5, 12).

Now or Later

How might our culture explain the Christian's internal struggle against the drag of the old nature? What direction from the world might actually do more harm in our lives than good?

7

Overcoming Death's Grip

2 Corinthians 5:1-10

As I walked to the pulpit to preach one Sunday, an usher handed me a note that a longtime church member had been taken to the hospital. We then prayed as a church family for this dearly loved man. When I visited his hospital room later that day, he told me that he wouldn't be around much longer. "I believe the Lord will take me home soon," he said. We talked a while longer and then prayed together. Tears burned my eyes as I left—not because I wanted to hold onto him, but because I would miss my friend. That night this faithful believer closed his eyes to all that surrounded him on Earth only to open them in the presence of Christ.

GROUP DISCUSSION. What death scene (either actual or from a book or movie) do you remember most vividly? Why did it make such an impact on you?

PERSONAL REFLECTION. What aspects of death or dying are most troubling to you? Spend a few minutes in prayer giving those concerns to the Lord.

Death is the appointed end for every human being. The Bible calls death the last enemy (1 Corinthians 15:26). God hasn't answered all our questions about what lies beyond death's door, but he has told us enough that we can face that final valley without fear. *Read 2 Corinthians 5:1-10.*

1. What feelings does reading this passage prompt in you—anticipation? fear? concern? Explain why you feel this way.

2. What does Paul mean by "the earthly tent we live in" (v. 1)?

What is this "earthly tent" like according to Paul (vv. 1-4)?

3. What is the alternative to our present "tent" and what is it like?

4. How does the presence of the Holy Spirit guarantee what is to come after death (v. 5)?

5. What is true of a believer who is "at home in the body," and why does that require a walk of faith (vv. 6-7)?

6. What is true of a believer who is "away from the body," and why does Paul prefer that condition (v. 8)?

How does this passage bring comfort and hope to us about Christians who have died?

7. Does Paul's confident declaration make you more secure or more insecure about death? Explain your answer.

8. What does Paul tell us about our future accountability to Christ (v. 10)?

_____

9. Does this mean we somehow have to answer for our sins?

_____

10. What hope can you offer a person who thinks death is the end of our existence?

Prayerfully consider whether you will face Christ with shame or with joy. Ask the Holy Spirit to direct you in ways you can be better prepared to meet the Lord with joyful anticipation.

Now or Later

Paul's knowledge of his future accountability pushed him to live in such a way that Christ was honored by his actions and motives. What is one step you can take this week to make your life more pleasing to the Lord? Talk about that goal with a Christian friend who will encourage you to live more obediently to Jesus.

8

Finding Hope in a Terrorized World

Psalm 46

During the dark days of the Reformation when Martin Luther's life was threatened and when the enemies of the gospel seemed strongest, the reformer would find his friend, Philipp Melanchthon, and say to him, "Let's sing the forty-sixth psalm." Luther loved this psalm because he believed God would defend his people against every assault. Luther even wrote a great hymn based on the psalm—"A Sure Stronghold Our God Is He" (better know to us as "A Mighty Fortress Is Our God").

GROUP DISCUSSION. What event has frightened or disturbed you most in the past twelve months? How did you cope?

PERSONAL REFLECTION. What refuge do you seek out when life seems to be caving in on you? To whom or to what do you turn *first* for comfort or security?

Psalm 46 was written as a song of deliverance. Perhaps God had rescued Israel from the attack of an enemy or from a plague of illness sweeping the region. Whatever the threat was, God demonstrated his power and his compassion by protecting his people. *Read Psalm 46.*

---

1. The author of Psalm 46 looks to God for two kinds of help. First, God is a refuge, a safe place where we can run for protection. He protects us *from* the storm. Second, God is a help, a source of inner strength when calamity or trouble breaks over us. He walks with us *through* the storm. In which way do you experience God's care most often? Share a personal example with the group.

---

2. The psalm is divided into three stanzas, each ending with the word *Selah,* which signaled a musical interlude to give the reader time to think about what had been said. As you think about it, what crisis or situation in your life could be described by verses 2 and 3?

---

3. Why are we not to fear in those desperate, uncertain times?

4. The second stanza (vv. 4-7) pictures the security and safety of dwelling in God's presence. How would you describe the place where you normally "dwell" spiritually? Is it near God or a distance away?

5. Where do you sense a need for God's fortress-protection in your experience right now?

6. Stanza three (vv. 8-11) looks beyond the present to the day in the future when all of God's enemies will be conquered. How does that truth help us when we feel like giving up or giving in?

7. What is involved in being still before God?

Why does that help us when we feel threatened?

8. What truths about God will you claim from this psalm when your world is terrorized?

---

9. As you think back through the studies in this LifeGuide, what questions about good and evil were answered for you?

Where do you still have concerns or doubts?

Talk to the Lord about the areas where you still doubt or struggle, and ask him to strengthen your trust and reliance on him as your refuge and help.

Now or Later

Memorize or write out verses 1-3 of Psalm 46, and put the passage where you tend to do the most worrying—on the dashboard, in the checkbook, next to pictures of your children. Learn to be still and think about God's goodness and protection when fear or uncertainty tries to grip your life.

Leader's Notes

MY GRACE IS SUFFICIENT FOR YOU. (2 COR 12:9)

Leading a Bible discussion can be an enjoyable and rewarding experience. But it can also be *scary*—especially if you've never done it before. If this is your feeling, you're in good company. When God asked Moses to lead the Israelites out of Egypt, he replied, "O LORD, please send someone else to do it" (Ex 4:13). It was the same with Solomon, Jeremiah and Timothy, but God helped these people in spite of their weaknesses, and he will help you as well.

You don't need to be an expert on the Bible or a trained teacher to lead a Bible discussion. The idea behind these inductive studies is that the leader guides group members to discover for themselves what the Bible has to say. This method of learning will allow group members to remember much more of what is said than a lecture would.

These studies are designed to be led easily. As a matter of fact, the flow of questions through the passage from observation to interpretation to application is so natural that you may feel that the studies lead themselves. This study guide is also flexible. You can use it with a variety of groups—student, professional, neighborhood or church groups. Each study takes forty-five to sixty minutes in a group setting.

There are some important facts to know about group dynamics and encouraging discussion. The suggestions listed below should enable you to effectively and enjoyably fulfill your role as leader.

Preparing for the Study

1. Ask God to help you understand and apply the passage in your

own life. Unless this happens, you will not be prepared to lead others. Pray too for the various members of the group. Ask God to open your hearts to the message of his Word and motivate you to action.

2. Read the introduction to the entire guide to get an overview of the entire book and the issues which will be explored.

3. As you begin each study, read and reread the assigned Bible passage to familiarize yourself with it.

4. This study guide is based on the New International Version of the Bible. It will help you and the group if you use this translation as the basis for your study and discussion.

5. Carefully work through each question in the study. Spend time in meditation and reflection as you consider how to respond.

6. Write your thoughts and responses in the space provided in the study guide. This will help you to express your understanding of the passage clearly.

7. It might help to have a Bible dictionary handy. Use it to look up any unfamiliar words, names or places. (For additional help on how to study a passage, see chapter five of *How to Lead a LifeGuide Bible Study,* InterVarsity Press.)

8. Consider how you can apply the Scripture to your life. Remember that the group will follow your lead in responding to the studies. They will not go any deeper than you do.

9. Once you have finished your own study of the passage, familiarize yourself with the leader's notes for the study you are leading. These are designed to help you in several ways. First, they tell you the purpose the study guide author had in mind when writing the study. Take time to think through how the study questions work together to accomplish that purpose. Second, the notes provide you with additional background information or suggestions on group dynamics for various questions. This information can be useful when people have difficulty understanding or answering a question. Third, the leader's notes can alert you to potential problems you may encounter during the study.

10. If you wish to remind yourself of anything mentioned in the leader's notes, make a note to yourself below that question in the study.

Leading the Study

1. Begin the study on time. Open with prayer, asking God to help the group to understand and apply the passage.

2. Be sure that everyone in your group has a study guide. Encourage the group to prepare beforehand for each discussion by reading the introduction to the guide and by working through the questions in the study.

3. At the beginning of your first time together, explain that these studies are meant to be discussions, not lectures. Encourage the members of the group to participate. However, do not put pressure on those who may be hesitant to speak during the first few sessions. You may want to suggest the following guidelines to your group.

☐ Stick to the topic being discussed.

☐ Your responses should be based on the verses which are the focus of the discussion and not on outside authorities such as commentaries or speakers.

☐ These studies focus on a particular passage of Scripture. Only rarely should you refer to other portions of the Bible. This allows for everyone to participate in in-depth study on equal ground.

☐ Anything said in the group is considered confidential and will not be discussed outside the group unless specific permission is given to do so.

☐ We will listen attentively to each other and provide time for each person present to talk.

☐ We will pray for each other.

4. Have a group member read the introduction at the beginning of the discussion.

5. Every session begins with a group discussion question. The question or activity is meant to be used before the passage is read. The question introduces the theme of the study and encourages group members to begin to open up. Encourage as many members as possible to participate, and be ready to get the discussion going with your own response.

This section is designed to reveal where our thoughts or feelings need to be transformed by Scripture. That is why it is especially important not to read the passage before the discussion question is asked. The passage will tend to color the honest reactions people would otherwise give because they are, of course, supposed to think the way the Bible does.

You may want to supplement the group discussion question with an icebreaker to help people to get comfortable. See the community section of *Small Group Idea Book* for more ideas.

You also might want to use the personal reflection question with your group. Either allow a time of silence for people to respond individually or discuss it together.

6. Have a group member (or members if the passage is long) read aloud the passage to be studied. Then give people several minutes to read the passage again silently so that they can take it all in.

7. Question 1 will generally be an overview question designed to briefly survey the passage. Encourage the group to look at the whole passage, but try to avoid getting sidetracked by questions or issues that will be addressed later in the study.

8. As you ask the questions, keep in mind that they are designed to be used just as they are written. You may simply read them aloud. Or you may prefer to express them in your own words.

There may be times when it is appropriate to deviate from the study guide. For example, a question may have already been answered. If so, move on to the next question. Or someone may raise an important question not covered in the guide. Take time to discuss it, but try to keep the group from going off on tangents.

9. Avoid answering your own questions. If necessary, repeat or rephrase them until they are clearly understood. Or point out something you read in the leader's notes to clarify the context or meaning. An eager group quickly becomes passive and silent if they think the leader will do most of the talking.

10. Don't be afraid of silence. People may need time to think about the question before formulating their answers.

11. Don't be content with just one answer. Ask, "What do the rest of you think?" or "Anything else?" until several people have given answers to the question.

12. Acknowledge all contributions. Try to be affirming whenever possible. Never reject an answer. If it is clearly off-base, ask, "Which

verse led you to that conclusion?" or again, "What do the rest of you think?"

13. Don't expect every answer to be addressed to you, even though this will probably happen at first. As group members become more at ease, they will begin to truly interact with each other. This is one sign of healthy discussion.

14. Don't be afraid of controversy. It can be very stimulating. If you don't resolve an issue completely, don't be frustrated. Move on and keep it in mind for later. A subsequent study may solve the problem.

15. Periodically summarize what the group has said about the passage. This helps to draw together the various ideas mentioned and gives continuity to the study. But don't preach.

16. At the end of the Bible discussion you may want to allow group members a time of quiet to work on an idea under "Now or Later." Then discuss what you experienced. Or you may want to encourage group members to work on these ideas between meetings. Give an opportunity during the session for people to talk about what they are learning.

17. Conclude your time together with conversational prayer, adapting the prayer suggestion at the end of the study to your group. Ask for God's help in following through on the commitments you've made.

18. End on time.

Many more suggestions and helps are found in *How to Lead a LifeGuide Bible Study.*

Components of Small Groups

A healthy small group should do more than study the Bible. There are four components to consider as you structure your time together.

Nurture. Small groups help us to grow in our knowledge and love of God. Bible study is the key to making this happen and is the foundation of your small group.

Community. Small groups are a great place to develop deep friendships with other Christians. Allow time for informal interaction before and after each study. Plan activities and games that will help you get to know each other. Spend time having fun together—going on a picnic or cooking dinner together.

Worship and prayer. Your study will be enhanced by spending time praising God together in prayer or song. Pray for each other's needs— and keep track of how God is answering prayer in your group. Ask God to help you to apply what you are learning in your study.

Outreach. Reaching out to others can be a practical way of applying what you are learning, and it will keep your group from becoming self-focused. Host a series of evangelistic discussions for your friends or neighbors. Clean up the yard of an elderly friend. Serve at a soup kitchen together, or spend a day working on a Habitat house.

Many more suggestions and helps in each of these areas are found in *Small Group Idea Book.* Information on building a small group can be found in *Small Group Leaders' Handbook* and *The Big Book on Small Groups* (both from InterVarsity Press). Reading through one of these books would be worth your time.

Study 1. Understanding the Human Condition. Romans 3:9-20.
Purpose: To explore the basic human problem of sinfulness before God.

Group discussion. You may want to bring a stack of front-section newspapers or recent news magazines (such as *Time* or *Newsweek*) to the group meeting. Browse through the headlines or cover stories as a group. Talk about how much of the news is good news and how much is bad news. What questions about God does the bad news raise? What does the bad news reveal about human beings?

Question 2. Before we can grasp our need to be rescued, we have to see how bad off we really are. Our culture does not like the concepts of personal sinfulness and separation from God, but the Bible declares them to be true.

Question 3. This passage makes it clear that no human endeavor can ever please God. Human beings may seem to do good things or live morally upright lives, but those actions do not earn merit with God. Only what emerges from faith will ever please God. We are declared right before God because of the merits of Christ, not because we have done good works.

Question 4. The most righteous people among us are the first to admit that they have failings. The fact is we all sin—we all fall short of God's standard of perfection. People may think they are good in their own eyes, but in God's eyes we are all separated from him by our acts of sin.

Question 5. The only reason we seek after God is because God was first seeking us. Fallen, sinful human beings are incapable of initiating any action of good toward God. Our good works are always a response to God's initiating work in us.

Question 6. Theologians call the Bible's teaching on the human condition the *total depravity* of humankind. This simply means that human beings in themselves are as lost as they can be. We have no capacity or desire in ourselves to seek God or to obey God. The only hope we have is that God in his grace will work first in us. His Spirit gives us the capacity to respond in faith and obedience back to him.

Question 7. No one is made right with God by keeping the law—or by living under the Ten Commandments. The problem is not with God's law (which is holy and good); the problem is in our hearts. We will fail to keep the letter or the spirit of the law and will demonstrate by that failure our inability to do good or to please God.

Question 8. The bent toward evil in each human being is restrained by God in a variety of ways—the human conscience, social pressure, civil and parental authority, threat of arrest. Whatever "good" emerges from our culture or society is all because of God's patience and grace toward all human beings, not because we in ourselves are striving to be good.

Question 9. The law reveals our failure to keep the law! We are made conscious and aware of our sin when we read God's commands to do or not to do certain things. We realize that we have already failed to reach the standard of the law and therefore are guilty before God.

The final questions will give you a good indication of the spiritual condition of each group member. The only way to be right with God is through faith in Jesus alone. We can never be made right by good deeds or religious rituals or sincere intentions.

Study 2. Dealing with Disaster. Job 1.
Purpose: To understand how God's goodness and power relate to natural and human disasters.

Group discussion. The purpose of this question is to get members of the group to be honest about hard issues. Do not try to answer each person's questions or even to defend God as the questions are raised. It's okay to let the questions linger unresolved. The study may help answer some of the issues that are raised, but some questions will never be answered in this life. God never fully explained to Job why he went through the tragic experiences recorded in Job 1.

Question 1. You might want to use a poster board or white board to mark off the various scenes on Earth and in heaven, and to record the characters who populate each scene.

Question 2. Satan does not bring up Job's name; God does! God allowed the testing to come into Job's life to bring Job to a new level of spiritual maturity and to uncover elements of pride in Job's character (Job 13:18-23; 31:35-37; 40:1-2; 42:6). Satan plays a role in Job's experience but only under God's control and direction.

Question 3. Satan is convinced that Job only serves God for what Job gets out of it. God has blessed Job and protected Job, and Satan's response is who *wouldn't* serve God for those kinds of benefits? He thought that the minute God took away the elements of Job's good life, Job would turn his back on God.

Question 4. Satan is a powerful adversary, and his strength is not to be underestimated. The fact remains, however, that he operates under the sovereign authority of God, and he can do nothing beyond the limits that God sets. Satan's attacks may come in our lives too, but we know that he only goes as far as God permits him to go.

Question 5. Satan shows Job no mercy. He removes everything swiftly and with maximum cruelty. Satan is a fierce enemy, bent on killing and destroying whatever he can.

Question 6. Disaster or loss does not come haphazardly into our lives. God has a purpose in allowing tragedy to touch us, but he may not always reveal that purpose to us. The proper response to unexplained suffering is not to ask why—why me? why this? why now?—but to continue to trust God and to yield to his wisdom in the trial.

Question 7. Job recognized God's hand and God's purpose in his trial. He did *not* say, "The LORD gave and Satan has taken away." He said, "The LORD gave and the LORD has taken away." In it all, Job spoke well of the character of the Lord.

Question 9. We still don't have all the answers about disaster or suffering. Why does God allow famine or devastating hurricanes? The traditional "problem of evil" raises questions about God's power and goodness.

- If God is good and all-powerful, why does he allow such bad things to happen?
- Maybe he is good but not powerful enough to stop them.
- Maybe he is powerful but not good.
- Maybe God doesn't exist at all, and these are just random, meaningless events.

The Bible's answer is that God is both good and powerful, but he allows these events for his own purposes.

Question 10. It's difficult to listen when you are in pain. What we need to look and listen for are not the reasons for our suffering. Those will rarely be explained. What we need to listen for are evidences of God's care and assurances of his love. We may find those in God's Word, in the gentle whispers of the Spirit, or in the love and support of God's people.

Study 3. Disability and the Goodness of God. John 9:1-7.

Purpose: To wrestle with the question of why God allows physical and mental disabilities.

Question 1. The disciples believed that deformity or disability was a direct consequence of some act of personal sin. Since the man's blindness was from birth, either it was punishment for his parents' sin or perhaps the man himself sinned while still in his mother's womb. The Jewish rabbis of Jesus' day taught that a baby's kicking in the womb was the evidence of personal sin committed before birth!

Question 2. Jesus' answer reveals that he did not make the same connection. These kinds of disabilities come on people because we live in a sin-cursed world, but they are not usually the direct consequence of some act of sin. The disciples looked to the past for an explanation of the man's blindness; Jesus looked ahead to the opportunity to display the glory of God.

Question 3. Obviously God will not heal or correct every deformity or disability. But every situation can take on redemptive qualities as God works through that person's condition to bring glory to himself.

Question 4. The quadriplegic may not walk away from the wheelchair, but he or she can give glory to God through a life transformed by his grace. The person afflicted with a disability can also be a channel for the work of God as they give witness to God's sustaining grace. They can also be a rebuke to the rest of us who find it so easy to complain about minor inconveniences.

Question 5. Jesus put the man through a process of healing in order to awaken faith in the man's heart. Jesus actually made him more blind than he was by smearing mud on his eyes, but he wanted the man to believe him enough to obey his directions and to believe that something good would result from his obedience to Jesus.

Question 6. Some disabilities result from poor choices—diving into a shallow lake and damaging your neck—or from sinful activities—taking illegal drugs while pregnant and the child is born with a birth defect. Some disabilities come from the wrong actions of others—the drunk driver who hits a teenager riding a bicycle. Most disabilities, however, come because we live in a world marked by sin and death. Disease, disability and deformity are all the outward signs of sin's presence and its destructive power.

Question 7. God takes ultimate responsibility for these human problems. He *could* prevent them all but he chooses not to. God's goodness is displayed in his compassion and mercy to those who struggle with such disabilities and his eventual healing of those who have trusted him when they receive a resurrection body.

Question 8. We can say that God knows the situation and that God has allowed the situation for his own purposes. God has not been unaware or mistaken in this event. We say that not as a cold, uncaring evaluation but with love and sensitivity. We can also add that God's heart is moved with compassion for the child or the person who is afflicted in this way.

Question 9. We can respond as Jesus did, not by looking back for the cause of the disability but by looking ahead at how God might work through that disability to bring glory to his name. We can also respond by showing compassion and by being a friend or help to that person or to their caregiver.

Study 4. Struggling with Sickness. James 5:13-18.

Purpose: To investigate what the Bible says about handling sickness as a Christian.

Question 1. James specifically asks, "Is any one of *you* [Christians] sick?" The sick person must also have access to the elders or spiritual leaders of a church. Furthermore the instruments used are spiritual in nature, not physical—prayer, confession, anointing with oil. These instructions are for the Christian family, not for humanity in general.

Question 2. These directions are to be followed when sick people seem to have no strength for recovery in themselves. James is not saying we should not see a doctor or take medication, but when those avenues do not lead to recovery, then anointing is an appropriate response. Anointing is a practice to be used for serious illness.

The Roman Catholic Church bases the practice of last rites or extreme unction on this passage. A person near death is anointed and committed to God.

Question 3. The initiative is taken by the sick person to call the elders. Once there, the sick person should explain why he or she has called for the elders and should ask them to follow James' instructions. The elders can then begin to ask appropriate questions about any unconfessed sin or an unrepentant spirit.

Question 4. The oil seems to be used here in a symbolic way. The elders are not administering medical help but are acknowledging to God that their hope for healing is in God alone. Anointing is accompanied by confession of sin and intense prayer, which are spiritual practices not medical procedures.

Question 5. James seems to say that prayer *will* raise up the sick one. The key is his phrase, "the prayer offered in faith." That seems to be a specific prayer energized in the elders by the Holy Spirit. If that prayer is given by God, the sick one will be raised up. In some situations, God does not give that prayer and the illness continues. It is not a prayer dependent on the faith of the elders or on the faith of the sick one but a prayer given to the elders as God chooses. James also seems to want to impress us with the need for continuing, faith-filled prayer. The words *pray* or *prayer* occur seven times in the passage.

Question 6. At times sickness can be the direct consequence of sin in a person's life. Confession has to be part of the whole anointing process. If genuine confession is made and if the sickness is part of God's discipline in the sick person's life, the illness will be removed. Be careful not to connect *all* sickness with personal sin. We may get sick for a variety of reasons.

Question 7. James is not talking about confession before the entire Bible study group! I think James is advocating that we confess our sins to those we injured by the sin or perhaps that we confess our sins to trusted friends who can help us maintain some accountability. We confess to God for forgiveness and cleansing; we confess to others for restoration of relationship and for the discipline of accountability. If unconfessed sin is the cause of the sickness, God will reveal that quickly to the sick one. James is not advocating a long, painful search for some minor sin. In the situations I have been involved with, the person knew immediately what the sin was.

Question 8. Sometimes we do not have from God because we do not ask. We should confidently ask God for his healing touch on a sick person and then explore every avenue in which God's answer might come. God may use medicine or surgery or a doctor's care or a change in lifestyle or the powerful touch of his hand to lift sickness from us.

Question 9. If another Christian becomes seriously sick, we can prayerfully suggest that they follow James's direction. I have written a booklet that helps in this process—*How Can I Pray When I'm Sick?* published by InterVarsity Press. It's available in print or as an electronic book (go to www.ivpress.com). Once you present the idea of anointing, give the person time to think and pray about it. Ask God to burden their hearts to obey his Word.

Study 5. Our Enemy in the World. Revelation 12:7-12.

Purpose: To expose the power and strategy of our adversary, the devil.
Group discussion. The purpose of this question is not to debate or correct everyone's perception of Satan. Let people share freely. You may want to record their responses on a white board or poster board.

Then you can transition to the study itself by explaining that this is an opportunity to explore what the Bible says about Satan. You may have a group member who questions the reality of a personal devil. Rather than engage in a lengthy debate, suggest that they look at the biblical information with an open mind.

Question 1. Be careful that the group doesn't get bogged down answering this question. Allow different views to be voiced and then add that Christian interpreters of Revelation hold to all three of the suggested views on when these events take place. Some believe this war in heaven took place in the long ago past. Others believe it is a description of the ongoing struggle between God and Satan. I am persuaded that it is an event that takes place in the future. Satan today has access to God's throne in heaven where he accuses believers constantly (see verse 10 and our previous study from the book of Job). In the future God will expel him from heaven permanently and confine Satan's activity to the Earth.

Question 2. The battle is clearly over access to God's heaven. Satan does not want that access taken from him because it signals the beginning of the end of his career. (Satan can read the Bible too!) Michael and his angels ultimately overcome Satan and his angels and force them to remain in Earth's realm.

Question 3. Satan as a dragon is fierce, powerful and difficult to control. John's description of Satan as a serpent takes the reader back to the Garden of Eden and to Satan's deception of Adam and Eve. The title "devil" points out Satan's moral depravity and twistedness, as well as his power of slander and destructive words. Satan is a title that reflects his cruelty and constant opposition to all that is good and godly. The final phrase pictures Satan's deceptive nature and his desire to lead people down the path that moves them away from God and toward eternal death.

Question 4. Satan is certainly the source of much of the evil in the world, especially the evil directed against God and God's people. Satan seems to use deception, lies and moral corruption as his primary instruments, but he is also capable of inciting violence and oppression. Jesus said that Satan was a murderer from the beginning (John 8:44).

Question 5. God has a purpose—even for the likes of Satan! God seems intent to let sin and Satan run their full course before they are separated from God's people forever. God is not the source or author of evil, but his eternal plan included the presence of evil and the necessity for human redemption.

Question 6. This question is not simply an invitation to speculation, but it reveals a person's understanding of where evil resides and how it permeates our world. Satan is not the *only* source of evil in the world. The world system provides the opportunity and outlet for sinful behavior. The flesh, the sinful nature within us, provides abundant motivation to do what is wrong or displeasing to God. The elimination of Satan would take away a powerful advocate and tempter toward evil, but it would not produce a society of righteousness and justice.

Question 8. Christians can overcome Satan's assaults "by the blood of the Lamb" and "by the word of their testimony." We gain victory over Satan by clinging to the redemption and forgiveness that God offers through faith in Christ. No accusation against us can stand because Jesus has paid the price for our sin on the cross.

Question 9. Part of standing strong against Satan's attacks involves an understanding of the abundance of God's grace to us in Christ and a willingness on our part to claim that grace by faith. We hide from Satan's assault in the shelter of God's love and forgiveness. Other images the Bible uses are to put on the armor of God or to rebuke the devil. We don't rebuke him in our authority but in God's authority.

Study 6. The Enemy Within. Romans 7:14-25.

Purpose: To come to grips with the power of our flesh, our embedded bent toward sin.

Question 1. There is no definitive answer to this question. Its purpose is to get the group to think about the realism of the passage. Some people will think Paul is too harsh; others will identify with Paul's self-evaluation. The truth is that even the most spiritually mature Christian still has areas of sin to conquer and to bring into full submission to Christ. We may look at others and think they are close to perfect; they would probably be the first to explain that they fail often.

Question 2. The law is not the problem; the problem lies deep within each one of us. One reason for Paul's struggle is that he does not fully understand (v. 15) the battle between his new desires and the remnants of the old life that still drag him down. Sometimes it is hard to sort out motives and desires—are they from God or from our sinful nature? Another reason for his inconsistent obedience is the power of sin still residing within him (v. 17).

Question 3. Paul is not shirking his responsibility for his own sin. He is simply trying to point out how strong the sinful nature can be. It can overpower our desires to do good and can only be counteracted by the power of the Holy Spirit who also lives within us as believers.

Question 4. You, as the group leader, may want to be the first to answer this question. Be sensitive that no one judges those who admit to an ongoing struggle in their life. Even Paul confessed that he didn't always walk at the level of obedience that he wanted.

Question 5. The only source of rescue from sin's power is the power of God. God the Holy Spirit will provide the strength to overcome daily temptation, but full victory will only come when we are released from this sin-dominated world.

Question 6. The Christian life requires a consistent reliance on the Holy Spirit and a daily commitment to a walk of obedience. We may fail in a particular area, but God provides forgiveness and cleansing and we press on in pursuit of a life of holiness. The one response to the struggle we can't be satisfied with is to give up or give in and say that we just can't overcome a particular sin or habit. God always provides the power to resist or escape temptation (1 Cor 10:13).

Question 7. Sometimes the best help comes from following Paul's example here in Romans 7. We can often help others by sharing our own personal experience in the struggle against sin. When a friend realizes that we struggle too, it may give him confidence to keep resisting or to rely on God's power to overcome a particularly difficult habit or pattern of sin. We can also remind our friends of God's promises and the available power of the Holy Spirit.

Question 8. The passage gives several insights into dealing with pressure or temptation to sin. Admitting the struggle honestly to God and to another trusted believer is a good place to start. Recognizing and acknowledging that this temptation comes from the flesh, the sinful nature, also helps us stand firm. Calling on God's power to help us resist the temptation focuses our attention on the one source of help that is always available and that will never fail.

Question 9. Memorizing or having available appropriate passages of Scripture can be a powerful reminder of all that God makes available to you to live a life of holiness and obedience. Regular accountability to trusted friends can be another way to prompt yourself to faithful obedience. Even pictures of your spouse or your kids or others in your study group can be reminders of the importance of a consistent, godly life.

Study 7. Overcoming Death's Grip. 2 Corinthians 5:1-10.

Purpose: To examine our natural fear of death in the light of God's promises about our future.

Question 1. Allow group members to answer this question without judgment or correction. The point is to let them express some of their genuine feelings. Hopefully, answers or clarifications of their concerns will come as the study itself unfolds.

Questions 2-3. It is clear that Paul is talking about our earthly bodies and comparing them to the eternal bodies that we will receive in heaven. Our earthly bodies are mortal and burdened because of sin; our heavenly dwellings will be eternal and full of life.

Question 4. The Holy Spirit is the down payment, the guarantee of all the good things to come. He makes the resurrection power of Jesus a reality in our daily experience now, and he assures our future transformation at the resurrection. If God has given us such a good gift as the Spirit now, what will prevent God from giving us the rest of the good things he has promised?

Question 5. Believers who are in the body are "away from the Lord" (v. 6) in the sense that we are not in Christ's visible presence. We do not see yet the reality of heaven. We accept God's promises about heaven purely by faith. We have complete confidence in what God tells us and we order our lives accordingly.

Question 6. Paul would prefer to be in Christ's presence but that would require him to be "away from the body" (v. 8). This verse is one of the clearest biblical references that those believers who die go directly to be with the Lord in conscious awareness and fellowship. We can be comforted by the fact that, while they are separated from us for a time, they are with the Lord.

Question 7. The prospect of facing Christ after death may make some people nervous. It might also present an opportunity to explore those feelings and to address some of the concerns. Are they insecure because they have never believed in Jesus or because they don't feel worthy or because they fear condemnation? Each response lets you deal with that particular group member's spiritual understanding.

Question 8. Only believers will appear at the judgment seat of Christ. The issue will *not* be salvation. We are saved by grace through faith in Christ alone. The judgment seat will be a time of evaluation. What did we do with the resources and gifts God gave us? To what extent did our lives honor Christ? We will receive eternal rewards based on Christ's evaluation.

Question 9. No Christian has to fear condemnation at the judgment seat. The full penalty for our sin was paid at the cross. If, however, we have failed to confess sin to God or have tried to hide sinful motives, those issues will be revealed and dealt with in front of Christ.

Question 10. Death is not the end of human existence according to the Bible. Those who have refused to receive God's gift of forgiveness will continue to exist too—but in a place of separation from God. The only hope for a person facing death or fearing death is to put their confidence for the future in Christ who will never abandon them and whose love will see them through even death's dark valley.

Study 8. Finding Hope in a Terrorized World. Psalm 46.

Purpose: To instill confidence in the Lord as the only source of security in a troubled world.

Introduction. You may want to design a group reading of Psalm 46 to involve everyone in reading the Scripture passage. One suggested arrangement can be downloaded from the InterVarsity Press website (www.ivpress.com) under the name of this study guide. Print enough copies for the group and assign reading parts. You may want to stand as you read in honor of God's Word. If your group is larger, assign a small group of readers to perform the Scripture reading for the entire group.

If your group members are familiar with Luther's hymn "A Mighty Fortress Is Our God," you might want to pass out copies and sing (or read) the words of the hymn as part of your study time.

Question 1. Not everyone will have an example to share with the whole group. Ask for volunteers and give them time to describe how God helped them in a specific situation.

Question 3. We are not to fear because God is our refuge, an ever-present help in trouble. Difficult times put what we believe to the test. Where do we turn first when our world seems to fall apart?

Question 4. The people of Israel in the Old Testament looked to Jerusalem as the place of safety because God was present in his holy temple. Christians can dwell in God's presence anywhere and at any time because God the Holy Spirit lives in us. The question is: do we desire to have a close relationship with God or do we keep God on the fringes of our lives?

Question 5. Answers will differ depending on each person's situation. Some group members may not be comfortable answering this question publicly. Give them a safe place to respond, but don't push for an answer if the person is uncomfortable.

Question 6. All of God's enemies will, someday, be put down. As strong as the assault against us may be, we know that ultimately God wins. No spiritual power can defeat us as long as we rest on God's strength and God's grace.

Question 7. Being still before God does not require a quiet mountain retreat or several hours of solitude. Being still before God means to focus our full attention on who God is and on what he has promised to do for those who trust in him. When we feel threatened or under attack, we can focus on God's presence as our helper and on God's truth as our security. Everything and everyone else may fail us or disappoint us, but God never will.

Question 9. Allow group members to answer honestly. You may want to conclude the study by praying specifically for each person and their personal areas of concern. Not every question about good and evil will be answered in this life, but our God is a completely reliable source of help and strength. Encourage the group to follow through with the Now or Later project.

Douglas Connelly is the senior pastor at Parkside Community Church in Sterling Heights, Michigan. He is also the author of Angels Around Us *(InterVarsity Press) and* The Bible for Blockheads *(Zondervan) as well as nine LifeGuide® Bible Studies.*

What Should We Study Next?

A good place to continue your study of Scripture would be with a book study. Many groups begin with a Gospel such as *Mark* (20 studies by Jim Hoover) or *John* (26 studies by Douglas Connelly). These guides are divided into two parts so that if twenty or twenty-six weeks seems like too much to do at once, the group can feel free to do half and take a break with another topic. Later you might want to come back to it. You might prefer to try a shorter letter. *Philippians* (9 studies by Donald Baker), *Ephesians* (11 studies by Andrew T. and Phyllis J. Le Peau) and *1 & 2 Timothy and Titus* (11 studies by Pete Sommer) are good options. If you want to vary your reading with an Old Testament book, consider *Ecclesiastes* (12 studies by Bill and Teresa Syrios) for a challenging and exciting study.

There are a number of interesting topical LifeGuide studies as well. Here are some options for filling three or four quarters of a year:

Basic Discipleship
Christian Beliefs, 12 studies by Stephen D. Eyre
Christian Character, 12 studies by Andrea Sterk & Peter Scazzero
Christian Disciplines, 12 studies by Andrea Sterk & Peter Scazzero
Evangelism, 12 studies by Rebecca Pippert & Ruth Siemens

Building Community
Fruit of the Spirit, 9 studies by Hazel Offner
Spiritual Gifts, 8 studies by R. Paul Stevens
Christian Community, 10 studies by Rob Suggs

Character Studies
David, 12 studies by Jack Kuhatschek
New Testament Characters, 10 studies by Carolyn Nystrom
Old Testament Characters, 12 studies by Peter Scazzero
Women of the Old Testament, 12 studies by Gladys Hunt

The Trinity
Meeting God, 12 studies by J. I. Packer
Meeting Jesus, 13 studies by Leighton Ford
Meeting the Spirit, 10 studies by Douglas Connelly

ALSO FOR SMALL GROUPS...

As well as over 70 titles in the popular *LifeBuilder* series, Scripture Union produces a wide variety of resources for small groups. Among them are:

- **WordLive** – an innovative online Bible experience for groups and individuals offering a wide variety of free material: study notes, maps, illustrations, images, poems, meditations, downloadable podcasts, prayer activities. Log on and check it out: www.wordlive.org
- **The Multi-Sensory series** – popular resources for creative small groups, youth groups and churches, with appeal for a wide range of learning styles and plenty of photocopiable pages.
- **Deeper Encounter** – for confident groups having a good understanding of Bible text, seven sessions in each title complete with CD audio tracks and photocopiable work sheets.
- **Essential 100** and **Essential Jesus** – 100-reading overviews of the Bible (Essential Bible) and the person and work of Jesus (Essential Jesus), with notes and helps, presented as a programme for individuals, small groups or whole churches.
- **Connect Bible Studies** – a range based on contemporary issues, looking at what biblical principles we might apply to understanding them.

SU publications are available from Christian bookshops, on the Internet, or via mail order. Advice on what would suit your group best is always available. You can:
- phone SU's mail order line: local rate number 08450 706 006
- email info@scriptureunion.org.uk
- log on to www.scriptureunion.org.uk
- write to SU Mail Order, PO Box 5148, Milton Keynes MLO, MK2 2YX

Scripture Union
USING THE BIBLE TO INSPIRE CHILDREN, YOUNG PEOPLE AND ADULTS TO KNOW GOD